# THE ESSENTIAL BOOK OF
# AYURVEDA

# THE ESSENTIAL BOOK OF
# AYURVEDA

—

### Secrets of ancient healing wisdom

## KONSTANTINOS TSELIOS

SIRIUS

**SIRIUS**

This edition published in 2023 by Sirius Publishing, a division of
Arcturus Publishing Limited,
26/27 Bickels Yard, 151–153 Bermondsey Street,
London SE1 3HA

ISBN: 978-1-3988-2611-3
AD008853UK

Printed in China

# Contents

Introduction ........................................... 6

Chapter One: The Principles of Ayurveda ............. 18
    The Three Doshas ................... 25
    Which is my Dosha? ................. 32
    The Six Tastes ..................... 40
    Agni, the Digestive Fire ........... 52

Chapter Two: Ayurveda and the Mind ............... 60
    What is my Triguna, Mental Type? .... 65

Chapter Three: Ayurvedic Therapies .................. 74
    Pancha Karma Therapy ............. 80
    Oil and Herb Therapy ............... 87
    Gem Therapy ...................... 93
    Meditation Therapy ................ 101
    Mantra Therapy ................... 104
    Massage Therapy .................. 110

Chapter Four: Ayurveda and Yoga ................... 116
    Ayurveda and the Seven Chakras ..... 121

Chapter Five: Ayurvedic Diet and Recipes ........... 126

Chapter Six: Life and Death in Ayurveda ........... 144
    The Afterlife ...................... 150
    Final Thoughts ................... 153

Index ............................................... 154

About the Author ................................... 158

Acknowledgements ................................. 160

# Introduction

The literal translation of the ancient Sanskrit word 'ayurveda' into English is 'science of long life', with 'ayur' meaning long life and 'veda' meaning science or wisdom. It's an ancient Indian system of living that isn't limited to just one health therapy, such as taking herbal medicines, but instead refers to a whole system of healthy living and spiritual well-being.

Ayurveda traces its roots back to *The Vedas*, which are the ancient scriptures of India and some of the oldest records of human knowledge. There are four ancient Vedic Sanskrit texts, *The Rigveda*, *The Yajurveda*, *The Samaveda* and *The Atharvaveda*. *The Vedas* are considered by Hindus to be 'apauruseya' which means they are authorless and 'not of man,' but are instead sacred texts which have come from the universal creator and have been heard by ancient sages during meditation.

The two major ancient Sanskrit texts which have survived and which form the basis of ayurveda are *The Charaka Samhita* and *The Sushruta Samhita*. These texts describe ancient theories about the human body and health, outlining the importance of diet, hygiene, education and prevention of disease.

*The Charaka Samhita* text describes ayurveda as, 'The science that indicates the appropriate and inappropriate, happy or sorrowful, conditions of living; what is auspicious or inauspicious for longevity, as well as the measure of life itself.'

These ancient Vedic texts also stress the importance of teamwork between the patient and the doctors and nurses, rather than in Western, allopathic medicine where perhaps too much importance is given to top-down advice from the physician, with the patient just accepting any treatment that is given and not playing a more active part.

## MIND, BODY AND SPIRIT

Ayurveda is a complete system of living that uses natural substances and foods to promote good health and which also takes into account the role of the mind and emotions when it comes to healthy living.

You'll also hear people talk about 'ayurvedic medicine' and in India there's a long-established professional structure in place and it can take up to seven years to qualify as an officially recognized ayurvedic doctor. There's also a huge pharmaceutical industry in India based on ayurvedic medicine, using natural products that have been scientifically tested.

Many of the ayurvedic doctors in India have their own gardens where they produce some of their own medicines, with some even having small factory set-ups. An ayurvedic doctor may sometimes undertake invasive procedures, but this is now fairly rare since many Indians just use natural ayurvedic products

to help treat or prevent illnesses such as cancer, with a fully ayurvedic lifestyle designed to reduce the chances of health problems in the first place.

## MY AYURVEDIC EXPERIENCE

One of the reasons I wanted to write this book is because of my own personal experience with ayurveda. I am a yoga and mindfulness teacher, originally from Greece but living in London, UK, for over 20 years. I have a strong connection with India and have visited many times over the past decades.

Ten years ago, while staying in Varanasi (also once known as Benares) in northern India, I met my own ayurvedic doctor, Virendra Verma. As well as having an established practice, he also produces his own ayurvedic medicines, from natural plants and herbs.

I had been told by some fellow travelers, as well as by some of my Indian friends, that I should try ayurvedic medicine and was recommended Virendra as a well-respected local practitioner. I initially undertook an ayurvedic treatment called 'pancha karma' which is effectively an ayurvedic detoxification program, with 'pancha' in Sanskrit meaning 'five' and 'karma' meaning 'action'. It was a five-step process including cleansing enemas, nasal application of herbs and daily massages with hot herbal oils. After the treatment, which took 20 days in total, I felt lighter, more clear-headed and healthier, a feeling which lasted for several months.

Following this first experience with ayurveda, I have relied on it on many occasions. Once I had an eye infection with *staphylococcus aureus* bacterium (also known as an MRSA infection; methicillin-resistant *staphylococcus aureus*) and this caused one of my eyelids to swell up and become partly closed.

I went to my ayurvedic doctor and he took three cloves of garlic, crushed them, and then put this pulp on the top of my eyelid. It was very painful at first but, following more applications of garlic over two days, my eyelid inflammation started to reduce. After a week it had gone completely and I was more than happy, having suffered from this eyelid inflammation for over three months.

## COMPLEMENTING MODERN MEDICINE

I have also combined ayurvedic treatments, as well as natural complementary medicines, with treatments from modern allopathic medicine.

Just under a decade ago, I was diagnosed with cancer and had surgery to remove a tumor, along with follow-up chemotherapy, all done in a very coordinated and professional way by the UK's National Health Service in South London. However, at the same time I also took natural ayurvedic health recipes, focusing on a healthy diet to rebuild my immune system after the chemo-therapy. I was originally diagnosed with Stage 4 cancer, which started in the bowel but had spread to the liver and lymph system, but I now have been cancer-free for eight years.

I think a more holistic approach to health and medicine, combining modern allopathic medicine with 'alternative' and natural comple-mentary treatments plus ayurveda, or other ancient practices such as acupuncture, can provide a much more effective overall result.

Of course, many ayurvedic doctors in India would say that ayurveda is a complete system in

its own right, with thousands of years of ancient wisdom behind it, so there is no need for modern Western medicine at all. From my own experience, though, I think a combination of the two can lead to the best results.

## CONFLICTS WITH MODERN MEDICINE

As someone bought up in the 'West', like many people I have naturally absorbed the modern, empirical, scientific view of life during my upbringing, but I have also spent a lot of time in India getting to know the ancient systems of ayurveda and yoga. So, this book is written from the perspective of someone who knows both ways of thinking and, while writing it, I have been conscious of the potential conflicts between the two.

There have been a few modern health trials which have focused on some of the treatments used in ayurveda, such as herbal remedies, and these have had mixed results, sometimes showing the ayurvedic medicines have a good effect and sometimes saying they have little effect.

I suspect the large drug companies behind some of these trials aren't too interested in promoting the benefits of alternative treatments, when they make their money from selling modern drugs. But, these sorts of modern scientific trials are ignoring the overall nature of ayurveda, which is its combination of the

spiritual and a focus on the mind as part of the overall treatment of the physical body.

With a Western perspective we might be cynical and call the mental effect of drugs the 'placebo effect', which actually shows how important the mind is when it comes to health. However, even that misses the point because, in ayurveda, it's not just the body and mind that are key, but it is also important that we tap into the spiritual and creative energies of the universe.

Trying to analyze ayurveda with modern scientific tools is a bit like trying to analyze the potency of Christianity by taking something like a Geiger counter into the Vatican. The modern, empirical science of the past few hundred years has deliberately

avoided the spiritual nature of existence, concentrating instead on concrete, physical evidence.

However, many people are now questioning this empirical, logical explanation of the world and are adopting the more open-minded thinking seen in sciences such as quantum physics, which considers the interconnectedness of everything. We are slowly moving away from the narrow scientific thinking, where everything has a definable cause-and-effect, and are moving towards a more flexible understanding of everything, pulling together different viewpoints instead of just concentrating on a single-minded approach.

This holistic trend is also becoming a factor in modern thinking around health and medicine. We no longer separate the body and mind into different categories when it comes to health and well-being, but modern treatments are now linking the two, realizing that mental problems such as stress and anxiety can also lead to physical problems. Increasingly, spiritual aspects are also being considered in treatments, with yoga and meditation being recommended by some Western doctors.

Personally, I don't just think about gods and religion when considering spirituality, but also to concepts like 'self-love' or love in general. This is an important part of a person's spiritual well-being, which also feeds into their physical well-being.

In my mindfulness teaching I help people to love themselves more, making them happier with themselves by using tools like meditation, so they don't have to rely on the likes of anti-depressant tablets.

Modern thinking around health is perhaps getting closer to the ancient ayurvedic 'complete' approach, with renewed interest in natural medicines and organic foods as well as a focus on mental and spiritual health.

The fact that you are reading this book probably means that you are also open to looking at alternative ways of living healthily. I hope to give you a fundamental understanding of ayurveda, so that you can start or continue your own journey of exploration. I will show you how you can apply ayurveda to your own life and, ultimately, I would recommend visiting a fully qualified ayurveda doctor for a full consultation and help with any illnesses.

I should also say that I am not medically qualified, either in Western allopathic or ayurvedic medicine, so the treatments listed in this book are aimed as a guide to show you what ayurveda typically involves. You should always consult your own physician, either your Western doctor or ayurvedic doctor, before undertaking new treatments, if only to make sure they don't clash with any existing treatments you may be having.

I was always careful to consult with my oncologist before taking any natural herbal therapies alongside my chemotherapy, since some strong herbs or other natural products can conflict with modern pharmaceutical drugs.

# CHAPTER ONE

# The Principles
# of Ayurveda

The principle of the five elements that come together to create the organic and inorganic worlds lies at the core of ayurveda. These five elements are earth (prithi), water (jala), fire (tejas), air (vayu) and ether (akash). Akash refers to what we might now called 'space' as in outer-space, and includes the atmosphere, sky and other open spaces, which can be referred to as ether.

These elements come together in every creature and every human, but in a varied combination for each person. Everyone is slightly different in their mixture of elements and how their body creates a balance between all of them.

Ayurveda, as a system of medicine and healthy living, seeks to balance these elements in different people, while at the same time recognizing that these differences are also an important part of an individual's constitution.

## AYURVEDA AND THE BODY

To recognize the way that these five elements play a part in the human body, ayurveda identifies three primary life forces, or humors, within the body, called vata, pitta and kapha. These are known as the three doshas and they determine how our bodies grow and also how they decay. A literal translation of the word dosha is 'that which causes things to decay'. When the doshas are out of balance in a person, this can be the cause of disease within the body.

We are all born with a particular combination of these doshas within our bodies and this is known as our innate, natural constitution or 'prakruti' in ayurveda.

Ayurvedic treatment seeks to correct any imbalances between the doshas in a person, using natural therapies and treatments. These can include herbal remedies, specific diet regimes, meditation, massages, yoga and purification — which we might today call detoxification.

When diagnosing a health issue, the starting point for an ayurvedic doctor is normally to establish the balance of a patient's individual doshas. The doctor will then tailor the treatment taking account this balance.

Once you are aware of your own make-up when it comes to the three doshas, you can also tailor your diet and lifestyle choices to take account of this.

## THE SEVEN TISSUES

Also important in ayurveda is the concept of the 'seven tissues' or 'dhatus' which are the different types of tissue that make up the human body. These are as follows:

### Rasa dhatu
is the skin layer of our bodies

### Mamsa dhatu
is all the muscle tissues within the body.

### Rakta dhatu
is the blood and all its components

### Meda dhatu
is all the fatty or adipose tissue in the body

### Asthi dhatu
is the bone tissue

### Majja dhatu
is the bone marrow and tissues
of the nervous system

### Shukra dhatu
is all the tissue of the
reproductive system

Due to their watery nature (a quality most associated with the kapha dosha), most of these tissues are seen as kapha dosha forms. Muscle tissue, skin, fat tissue, bone marrow and reproductive tissues are all seen as kapha dosha tissues.

With its porous nature leaving space for air (a quality associated with the vata dosha), bone is seen as a vata dosha

tissue. Blood is seen as a pitta dosha tissue, partly because it circulates heat in the body (fire and heat are seen as pitta qualities).

Depending on a person's dosha type, they are mainly affected by diseases that relate to the tissue types specific to their dosha. So, vata illnesses are often related to the bones, pitta illnesses to the blood and kapha illnesses related to all the other bodily tissues.

That's not to say that people with one dosha type won't get the illnesses associated with another dosha. They are just more likely to suffer from the diseases associated with their own particular dosha.

In ayurvedic thinking, all the bodily tissues are supplied with their life force through channels or 'srotamsi' in the body. These are energy flows rather than specific, physical flows such as the blood system. Disease occurs when these channels become disrupted or blocked, often caused by an excess in one or more of the doshas. An ayurvedic doctor may examine these channels and their energy flows when diagnosing an illness.

# The Three Doshas

To begin using ayurveda and its various therapies, it is important to have a complete understanding of the three doshas, which determine how our bodies grow and also how they decay. When the doshas are out of balance in a person, this can lead to illness.

An ayurvedic doctor will first determine what a person's predominant dosha is, as well as looking at the proportion of the other doshas, before recommending treatment. A bit later on in the book I have included a guide to help you define your own predominant dosha, but first let's look at each of the three doshas individually.

## VATA DOSHA

The vata dosha is the 'air' humor and, like the wind, it relates to the force which moves things. The vata dosha is the driving force behind the other doshas, which would be immobile without it. Vata controls mental balance and promotes comprehension of the world around us.

Different qualities are given to each dosha and vata has the attributes of dry, light and cold. Each dosha exists within certain places in the body and the vata dosha is contained in the air or ether parts, filling up the empty spaces in the body. Specifically, it is said to rest in the colon, ears, bones, hips and our sense of touch. The primary site for vata is in the colon, where air can be produced as gas during the digestive processes.

As it is the driving force behind the other doshas, vata is seen as the primary dosha, responsible for all biological and physical processes. The way we care for this life force is important to our overall health.

Vata sustains exhalation and inhalation in our bodies, as well as controlling waste materials and maintaining our body tissues. It is also the basis for the coordination of our senses.

An excess of vata in the body has several symptoms and can lead to illness. The symptoms of excess vata can include loss of weight, insomnia, constipation, dizziness, confusion and shivering or body tremors.

As with the other doshas, vata can also be broken down into five different types. These are prana, udana, vyana, samana and apana. Prana is the primary air, contained within the brain and moving down to the chest, governing our minds, senses, heart and consciousness.

Udana is the air which moves upwards, in the chest and throat, which controls exhalation and speech. It is responsible for our aspirations in life and can be developed to give us psychic powers.

Vyana is the pervasive air, centered at the heart and spread all over the body. It controls the circulatory system and the movement of muscles and joints.

Samana is the equalizing air, based in the small intestine, and is the force which controls our digestive system.

Apana is the air which moves downwards and is centered in the colon, controlling waste processes such as urination, as well as menstruation and sexual activities.

Many ayurvedic doctors will say that treatment of apana is one of the main ways to deal with health problems relating to vata. Being the downwards moving force it can cause problems if it is aggravated or if there are blockages. This could take the form of colon problems such as constipation.

## PITTA DOSHA

The pitta dosha is the 'fire' humor and it relates to digestion. It controls metabolism and also our mental ability to digest facts and perceive things as they are.

The qualities given to pitta dosha are light, hot and moist. Within the body it exists as oil or water, or often as an acid form, hence the link to fire or heat.

Pitta is said to exist specifically in the small intestine, stomach, blood, lymph system and sebaceous glands. Its main site is in the small intestine.

Pitta controls the digestive system and aspects such as hunger and thirst, as well as governing heat within the body. It also controls intelligence and understanding.

An excess of pitta can cause problems with urine or waste matter as well as creating excessive hunger or thirst. It can also show up as a burning sensation as well as eye or skin problems.

Pitta is also broken down into five different types, namely sadhaka, alochaka, bhrajaka, pachaka and ranjaka. Sadhaka is the fire that relates to truth and reality and is located in the heart and brain. It allows us to achieve our goals in life, including material goals such as wealth and pleasure. It controls our mental digestion of information and concepts. Alochaka controls our visual perception and how we take in light and is based in our eyes. It also has an impact in the accuracy of other senses. Bhrajaka is the fire that controls our skin and maintains its condition, as well as controlling how we absorb heat through our skin. Pachaka is the fire that relates to our digestive system and is located in the small intestine. It is the primary type of pitta and the basis for the other types, so an ayurveda doctor will often consider this first when treating a pitta health issue. Banjaka is located in the liver, stomach and small intestine and is the fire that relates to colour, giving colour to the blood, bile and waste matter. It is based mainly in the blood and is often related to problems with the liver.

## KAPHA DOSHA

The kapha dosha is the 'water' humor which can also be thought of as phlegm. It supports most of our bodily tissues, holding everything together. It also relates to 'holding together' emotional traits such as love and compassion, providing an emotional support structure as well as a physical one.

The qualities given to kapha dosha are cold, heaviness and moisture. Within the body it exists as water, held within our skin and as mucus or phlegm.

Within the body, kapha is located specifically in the throat, head, chest, pancreas, stomach, lymph system, nose and as fat. Its main location is in the stomach.

Kapha is responsible for lubrication of the body and holding it all together and mentally it relates to the qualities such as patience.

An excess of kapha can result in nausea, lethargy, heaviness, difficult breathing and a constant feeling of tiredness. Problems with the joints and skin may also arise. Kapha dosha is also broken down into five different types, namely, tarpaka, bodhaka, avalambaka, kledaka and sleshaka. Tarpaka is located in the brain and is a form of water that leads to contentment, controlling emotional stability and happiness as well as our memory.

Bodhaka is the type of water that is located in our mouths as saliva which enables us to taste food. It is the first stage in the digestive process, lubricating the system.

Avalambaka is located in the heart and lungs and is the water in the form of phlegm that lubricates the body, distributed by the actions of the lungs and the heart.

Kledaka is located in the stomach and is the water that moistens, primarily as the secretions from the lining of the stomach that help to digest food.

Sleshaka is the type of water that provides lubrication around the body, such as in the joints, maintaining them and keeping them working.

# Which is my Dosha?

To be able to apply ayurvedic treatments to yourself, the starting point is to find out which is your dominant dosha. Once you have established this you can devise a life plan, which might include a certain type of diet, physical exercise such as yoga asanas, meditation or herbal treatments, all designed to help you to live a healthier and longer life.

Some people have one dosha which is very dominant but others will have a mixture of types, either with two dominant or with a mixture of all three doshas.

Three different types of dual dosha exist, either vatta-pitta, vata-kapha or pitta-kapha. Those who have a fairly equal level of all three doshas are referred to as the VPK type.

So, if you add all the above types together with the single dosha types, then there are seven possibilities for your individual dosha make-up. When it comes to treatment of illnesses, a balanced way is often to target the doshas that you are low on, or lacking. So, for instance, someone who has a vata-kapha constitution should aim to increase their pitta dosha.

The following questionnaire is designed to help you establish your own dosha constitution. See which description best applies to you for each category and then add up all the scores at the end. You may find that more than one description applies to you for each category, so just give a score for each.

Once you have finished, total up all the scores and see which is your dominant dosha, plus you'll find out if you have a mixture of them and in what ratios.

Later in the book you can then think about your own dosha constitution when it comes to the various ayurvedic treatments, remedies and foods, perhaps concentrating on the dosha you are lacking or reducing excess in your existing doshas.

## DOSHA QUESTIONNAIRE

Decide if you are vata, pitta or kapha dosha for each of the following categories, then mark your type for each category. In some categories you may feel that you comply to more than one dosha so select a couple of doshas if this is the case.

At the end, add up all your scores to find out which is your predominant dosha or what combination of doshas you have.

| Category | Vata |
| --- | --- |
| Body shape | Thin and either tall or short in height |
| Face shape | Long, angular face with hollow cheeks and small, set-back eyes |
| Skin quality | Fairly thin, dry skin which can be rough |
| Hair quality | Coarse, dry hair which may be wiry or curly |
| Hands | Small hands which can be fairly cold |
| Feet | Small, thin feet that can be rough |
| Teeth | Small and crooked teeth, slightly receding gums |
| Nails | Thin and often quite rough nails |
| Legs | Thin legs with prominent knees |
| Body strength | Fairly weak with poor endurance |

| Pitta | Kapha | score (V, P, K) |
|---|---|---|
| Medium build with a well-proportioned physique | Fairly stocky build with well-developed physique | |
| Angular face shape with smooth cheeks, a long nose and bright eyes | Rounded face with a small nose and large eyes | |
| Oily skin which is moist and may have moles or spots | Fairly thick, smooth skin with good moisture content | |
| Fine or medium quality, light, oily hair | Thick hair that may be oily and curly | |
| Medium size hands that are warm | Large hands that can be thick and oily | |
| Medium size soft feet | Large, thick feet which can feel hard | |
| Good size teeth with normal gums | Large teeth and thick gums | |
| Good quality nails, quite smooth | Large, thick nails, smooth and firm | |
| Average-size legs | Thick, stocky legs | |
| A reasonable level of sporting endurance | Good strength and endurance but can be slothful | |

| Category | Vata |
| --- | --- |
| Sex drive | Erratic sex drive, enjoy fantasies, may have few children |
| Appetite | Variable and erratic appetite, often feeling hungry |
| Taste preferences | Like spicy foods and enjoy snacking |
| Thirst | Fairly variable |
| Digestive system | Variable digestion, both good and bad |
| Bowel movements | Can be irregular and hard or constipated |
| Resistance to disease | Poor resistance with fairly weak immune system |
| Personality | Very creative, imaginative and artistic |
| Personal expression | Talk quickly, often without thinking first |
| Memory | Good short-term memory but long-term is not so good |

| Pitta | Kapha | score (V, P, K) |
|---|---|---|
| A good, passionate sex drive | A steady sex drive, may have many children | |
| A good, strong appetite and like regular meals | A reasonable appetite and enjoy eating | |
| Like foods that are not too spicy and high in protein | Like foods that are fatty and full of carbohydrates | |
| Often very thirsty | Usually not very thirsty | |
| Good digestion with few problems | Digestion usually good but can be a little slow | |
| Regular bowel movements with loose stools | Regular, heavy bowel movements | |
| Reasonable disease resistance | Good resistance to illness | |
| Logical and focused on finding solutions | Good natured and generous, like helping others | |
| Fairly confident and articulate | Thoughtful and considered when speaking | |
| Good overall memory, both short and long | Can be forgetful but with good long-term memory | |

| Category | Vata |
|---|---|
| Leader or follower | Often prefer to work alone but can take the lead if needed |
| Communication | Like to speak quickly and often erratically |
| Mental outlook | Don't stick to routines and can be chaotic in nature |
| Opinions | Tend to be fluid and change your opinions quite often |
| Emotional nature | Anxious and nervous |
| Sporting nature | Like active, fast-paced sports and activities |
| Sleeping | Tend to be a light sleeper and have trouble sleeping |
| Dreams | Restless dreams full of activities such as flying |
| Finances | Tend to spend money quickly and without thought |

| Pitta | Kapha | score (V, P, K) |
|-------|-------|-----------------|
| Like to be in charge and can be a good leader | Prefer following others and are easy to get along with | |
| Good communicator and listener | Quiet, considered and slow speaker | |
| Like routines but can be flexible if needed | Enjoy a set routine and don't like changes | |
| Have your own opinions but also listen to others | Have strong opinions and don't change your mind often | |
| Sometimes irritable and argumentative | Calm and contented | |
| Enjoy interaction and competition with others | Often prefer more individual-based sports and activities | |
| Enjoy reasonable sleep and usually feel restored after | Heavy, sound sleeper, find it hard to wake up | |
| Vivid dreams with striking visual images | Sentimental dreams, often about loved ones | |
| Have a planned approach to spending | Tend to like saving and holding on to money | |
| | **Final Total** | |

# The Six Tastes

When it comes to ayurvedic herbal or diet treatments, as well as the consideration of a person's dosha constitution, an ayurvedic doctor will also consider the 'six tastes'. These are sweet, salty, sour, pungent, bitter and astringent.

In Sanskrit, these tastes are called the 'rasas' and in ayurvedic medicine these tastes are considered as each consisting of two of the five elements; earth (prithi), water (jala), fire (tejas), air (vayu) and ether (akash). So, for instance, the sweet taste, from sugars and starches, is considered to be made up of earth and water and has a cooling energy.

Depending on your particular dosha, these tastes can either increase or decrease on your dosha level and an ayurvedic doctor will bear this in mind when prescribing diet or treatment. As an example, sweet tasting foods will decrease vata and pitta but increase kapha, so an ayurvedic doctor might prescribe sweet tasting foods to increase and create a better balance vata and pitta in a patient.

I'll give a full breakdown of the six tastes here, so you can see how they relate to each dosha.

## SWEET TASTE

Sweet taste is made up of the elements of earth and water, it has a cold energy, is usually oily and heavy, and will decrease pitta and vata, but increase kapha. Therefore, it is good for balancing pitta and vata.

In moderation, the sweet taste will build strength and is good for growth of muscles, blood, fat cells and bones. It can increase the health of skin and hair and relieve thirst.

With a cold energy, it is good for balancing burning sensations and can aid digestion. It is needed in fairly high quantities for all dosha types, especially pitta and vata and is important for growth of the cells and tissues of the body.

Excessive use of the sweet taste can lead to heaviness, laziness, obesity, congestion and loss of appetite. In extremes it can lead to diabetes and even encourage the growth of tumors.

Sweet taste is typically found in foods that are high in sugars and starches, such as rice and cereals, dried fruits milk and maple syrup.

## SALTY TASTE

Salty taste is made up of the elements of fire and water. It has a hot energy and will increase kapha and pitta but reduces vata.

Too much salty taste may aggravate kapha and pitta but it may help vata.

The salty taste can stimulate digestion but in large amounts can cause vomiting. It can help to cleanse the body tissues and increase absorption of minerals. It is necessary for all dosha types in small quantities as it helps with water retention and is necessary for bodily functions.

Salty taste is found naturally in some sea weeds and olives, as well as in sea salt or rock salt

## SOUR TASTE

Sour taste is made up of the elements of earth and fire. It has a hot energy and is normally liquid and oily in nature. It will

increase pitta and kapha, but reduce vata. Pitta is the most increased by the sour taste.

The sour taste is a stimulant to appetite, digestion and saliva production and can help with the release of gas. It can energize and nourish body tissues but an excess can irritate the body and mind. All doshas require small amounts of the sour taste as it helps with the acid balance in the body, but more is needed for vata with less for kapha and pitta.

Excessive amounts of the sour taste can cause thirst, hyperactivity, heartburn, indigestion and ulcers. Fermented foods can be toxic in the blood system and can cause skin problems such as psoriasis, eczema and acne. The acid quality of the sour taste can cause burning sensation, not just with heartburn but also in the bladder and in the throat.

Sour taste is found in foods such as vinegar, lemon and other citrus fruits, yogurt, cheese, wine plus fermented and picked foods.

## PUNGENT TASTE

Pungent taste is made up of the elements of fire and air. It has a hot energy and is usually light and drying. It will increase pitta and vata but decrease kapha. Pungent foods can be used to balance kapha but can aggravate pitta and vata if used in excess.

The pungent taste is a stimulant and can encourage sweating, by heating up the body and speeding up digestion. It can help with blood circulation and also aid quick thinking and mental awareness. It is also necessary in small amounts for all the doshas, helping with appetite and digestion, but more is necessary for kapha than the others.

Excessive amounts of the pungent taste can cause problems with the reproductive system, such as reducing or killing

sperm and ova. It can also cause fainting, fatigue and burning sensation such as heartburn, as well as creating nausea. Other symptoms include insomnia and body shaking, with vata particularly prone to problems of excessive pungent taste.

The pungent taste is found in foods such as ginger, onions,

garlic, mustard plus hot peppers and some hotter spices such as cayenne pepper.

## BITTER TASTE

Bitter taste is made up of the elements of air and ether. It has a cold, light and dry energy. It will increase vata but decrease kapha and pitta. It is best for treating and reducing pitta and kapha.

The bitter taste is cleansing and detoxifying, removing waste from the body with its cooling energy. It can kill germs in the body and can help to relieve burning sensations and help with skin problems. It may also help with mental purification and cleansing, freeing you from bad thoughts or emotions. It is necessary in small amounts for all the doshas as it helps with weight reduction and detoxification, but more is needed for pitta than for the other doshas.

Excessive amounts of the bitter taste may cause problems with muscles, bone marrow and fat cells. It can also lead to dryness and roughness of the skin and can cause weariness.

The bitter taste is found in foods such as raw green vegetables, turmeric, dandelion root, rhubarb and coffee, as well as in black teas or green teas.

## ASTRINGENT TASTE

Astringent taste is made up of the elements of earth and air. It has a cold, dry and heavy energy. It will increase vata but decrease pitta and kapha. Pitta can benefit most from the astringent taste but it can also be used to balance kapha.

The astringent taste can help with healing, particularly of the skin, and can help to reduce bodily discharges such as sweating and diarrhea but can cause the build-up of gasses in some people if taken in excess. It can help to stop bleeding by promoting blood clotting and can also help with healing ulcers. It is needed in limited quantities by all doshas but is needed most by pitta.

Excessive amounts of the bitter taste can cause constipation, dryness of the mouth and voice problems, as well as convulsions or emaciation in extreme cases. It can also lower the sex drive, reducing the levels of sperm produced.

The astringent taste is found in foods such as green beans, cranberries, grapes, unripe bananas, turmeric, okra, chickpeas, pomegranate plus teas that contain tannin.

## HOW THE SIX TASTES AFFECT THE DOSHAS

Depending on your dosha, it is important to get the right balance between all the six tastes in your daily diet, or when treating illnesses. Too much of any particular taste will aggravate the particular dosha or doshas that it is known to increase, but in great excess it can even aggravate the dosha that it is known to reduce.

Each taste has its own power, so some must be taken moderately for all doshas. The salty, bitter and pungent tastes are the strongest so will usually be taken in relatively small quantities. The astringent and sour tastes have more limited power so will need to be taken in greater quantities if they are to affect the doshas. The sweet taste is the least powerful when it comes to affecting the doshas, so may need to be taken in greater quantities.

When you consider that carbohydrates form a large part of most people's diets, you can see that it's not hard to eat big quantities, but kapha dosha people need to take care and reduce the sweet taste in their diet.

A lack of any of the tastes can also cause problems, according to your dosha. So, with the example of the sweet taste, vata and pitta types will suffer if they don't have enough of the sweet taste in their diet, but even a kapha type will suffer if they have hardly any of the sweet taste in their diet.

With our craving for carbohydrates and sugars being targeted by the modern food industry, this taste is normally a big part of most people's diets, but bitter, astringent and pungent tastes are much less used, so many of us could do with increasing these.

The six tastes come as either part of complex foodstuffs or in their pure form. The pure form of sweet is refined sugar, the pure form of salty taste is refined or natural salt, a pure form of the sour taste is alcohol, a pure form of the pungent taste is hot peppers and the powder made from them, a pure form of the bitter taste is found in some raw vegetable extracts and a pure form of the astringent taste is found in strong teas with tannin.

Some of these pure forms of taste can be used in treatments and ayurvedic doctors may use them in pills or other medicine forms. In India there's something called the 'six tastes pill' which deliberately combines all of the tastes in one pill and which is often given to children, in the same way that Western allopathic medicine might perhaps recommend vitamin tablets for children.

In adults, the 'six tastes pill' is sometimes used to help stimulate the entire digestive process and absorption of foods. The exact formulation of this pill is often tailored to specific dosha types, so perhaps with less of the sweet taste for kapha types.

## COMBINING THE SIX TASTES

As well as with the six tastes pill, combining any of the six tastes when preparing food can help create a healthy, balanced diet. A good combination of two or more of the tastes will probably be part of most popular dishes anyway, because this can result in better digestion. A dish wouldn't have become popular in the first place if it was known to cause indigestion!

Good food combinations in ayurveda include mixing a sweet taste with a pungent taste. Here, the sweet taste will help reduce the burning nature of the pungent taste and help the body to digest it. So, effectively, adding something sweet to a spicy dish can make it easier to digest. With the sweet taste seen as having a cold nature in ayurveda and pungent taste having a hot nature, then their combination creates a food that has a more balanced nature and is easier to digest.

As well as combining the six tastes to create a better balance, they can also be mixed together to create the opposite effect, making them more potent together than they would be individually. This can be important for ayurvedic doctors when producing medicines or recommending foods to reduce the level of one of the doshas or increase the level of a dosha that is lacking.

So, for instance, the pungent taste and the astringent taste are both known to reduce the kapha dosha, so combining them in the right way will have an even stronger effect on reducing kapha. Something like ginger could be used to provide the pungent taste and a tannin-rich tea could be used to provide the astringent taste, so the resulting ginger tea would be a good way to reduce kapha.

Sometimes the combination of similar foods doesn't work because they can overload your digestive system. For example, too many different types of proteins in one dish can make it hard to digest, such as combining fish, with cheese and beans. However, something like yoghurt, which contains protein, can normally be added to high-protein meals because it aids digestion.

The other thing to consider when combining the six tastes is the weight and liquid strength of each taste. The sweet taste, salty taste and astringent taste are all heavy in nature, with sweet being the heaviest. The sour, pungent and bitter tastes are all seen as lighter in nature, with bitter being the lightest.

When it comes to their liquid nature, sweet, salty and sour are the wettest, with sweet as the wettest. The drier tastes are astringent, bitter and pungent, with pungent as the driest.

So, when creating a dish that has a good balance, you may want to balance a heavy taste with a light one and a wet taste with a dry one, while at the same time taking into account the impact on your dosha type. For example, something like a spicy sweet-and-sour vegetable dish would combine the heavy and liquid sweet taste with the lighter sour taste and the spice would provide the pungent taste which has a dry nature.

The impact of this dish on, for example, the kapha dosha would be that the sweet taste increases kapha, the sour taste also increases kapha but the pungent taste reduces kapha. The limited quantity of the spice normally used in such a dish would probably mean that, overall, this is a dish that would increase kapha. It would have the opposite effect on the vata dosha, as both the sweet and sour tastes reduce vata, while only the pungent spice would increase vata.

# Agni, the Digestive Fire

As well as the six tastes, ayurveda also places great importance on the concept of the 'digestive fire' which is referred to as 'agni'. In the Hindu religion, Agni is the god of fire who is the protector of humanity as well as the protector of home. Various types of fire are associated with agni, such as the domestic fire used for cooking, small fires that burn incense and are used for Hindu prayers, as well as the fire of the funeral pyre.

The digestive fire is also referred to as agni because it is seen as 'the transforming force' within our bodies and this has a spiritual nature as well as what we would now call a biological function.

In ayurveda, eating healthily isn't just about the correct balance of foods we take into our bodies when it comes to the doshas, and aspects such as the six tastes, but it is also about how well our body is prepared when it comes to digesting and taking the nutrients out of this food and making use of them.

In modern terms, agni would include everything we think of under the headings of digestion, absorption, metabolism and egestion/excretion from the body. In ayurveda, having a good agni is seen as the most important thing when it comes to

overall health, with most health problems stemming from bad agni as this will reduce resistance to disease as well as cause its own problems which might manifest as skin conditions or lack of energy.

If a person's agni is not good then some of the food which is ingested will not be digested properly, leaving undigested food within the body. In ayurveda, this undigested food is seen as a toxic substance and referred to as 'ama'.

A build-up of too much ama can lead to diseases of many types, along with an overall feeling of being run-down and tired all the time. Other symptoms could include constipation or diarrhea and indigestion, possibly leading to mental confusion and depression.

There are four different states or levels of agni in ayurveda, as follows:

**The sama agni, or balanced agni,** is where a person has a normal appetite and regular bowel action. All their doshas will be in a good balance for their particular dosha constitution. They will have a good immune system and also be clear minded and happy.

**The vishama agni, or variable agni,** is where appetite is very variable, swinging from periods of extreme hunger to total loss of appetite. Symptoms can include diarrhea or constipation and a general feeling of heaviness after food. It can lead to skin problems and even insomnia, leading to an anxious mental state. The vishama agni is normally associated with vata dosha types, where the cold quality associated with vata can impact agni.

**The manda agni, or low agni,** is where appetite is poor, metabolism is slow and there's a tendency to put on weight. Symptoms can include general heaviness, loss of appetite and lethargy, with obesity and diabetes often a problem. The body will feel weak and the mind can be very possessive, attached to people and possessions. The manda agni is associated most with the kapha dosha type, where the heavy, slow and cold nature of kapha can lower the agni. Most of the illnesses associated with the kapha dosha will be linked to this low agni.

**The tikshna agni, or high agni,** is where there is an excessive appetite, with the consumption of large meals often leading to problems such as heartburn. Problems can also include diarrhea. Mentally, high agni can lead to feelings of anger and hate, making someone very critical of others.

Overall, resistance to disease is good and tikshna agni is most associated with the pitta dosha type, where the hot nature of pitta can fire up the agni.

## STIMULATING GOOD AGNI

As a whole, the digestive fire, agni, is seen as having a hot and dry energy in ayurveda. Treatments to stimulate agni will often involve spices, which are also seen as hot and dry. Generally, agni is stimulated with the salty, sour and pungent tastes but reduced with the bitter, sweet and astringent tastes.

The spices frequently used in ayurveda to increase agni include ginger and hot peppers such as cayenne or just black pepper. A frequently used ayurvedic treatment to increase agni is a formula which mixes ginger, coriander, nutmeg, black pepper, clover and Indian long pepper, all in equal quantities. This mixture can then be taken in small quantities, mixed with water before every meal, to stimulate agni. It can be very helpful for people with low or variable agni.

For those with high agni, foods which are sweet and oily can be used to reduce this. Changing your lifestyle so that you relax and sleep more can also help to reduce the digestive fire.

## THE DIGESTIVE PROCESS

In ayurveda, the digestive process is also explained in relation to the doshas. The digestive process begins in the mouth, where enzymes in the saliva, together with the process of chewing, begin to digest the food. The enzymes in saliva start the process of breaking down starches and sugars, with the alkaline nature of the saliva creating the right PH (acid/alkaline) balance for this process. For this reason, if a starchy food such as bread is eaten at the same time as an acidic food like a citrus fruit juice, then the process of breaking down starches is slowed and can even lead to indigestion.

This initial stage of digestion, in the mouth and stomach, is seen as one which is dominated by the kapha dosha. People who have kapha dosha may produce too much of the excretions that control digestion, such as saliva and mucus. Eating too much of the sweet taste or salty taste may increase these secretions even further, causing digestion to slow down.

The next stage of digestion. moving from the stomach to the small intestine, is seen as a process that is dominated by the pitta dosha, with the acid environment having the fire that is related to pitta. This acid environment can become even stronger if foods which have the pungent or sour taste are eaten in excess, leading to heartburn and indigestion.

The final stage of digestion, in the large intestine, is seen as a vata process in ayurveda. Vata is the air dosha and the large intestine is the place where many of the gasses of the digestive process are created. These can occur in excess in vata types and consumption of the pungent or astringent taste can make them worse, also leading to constipation.

As well as the amount and types of food eaten, the order in which they are eaten can also be important for good digestion. In the Western diet, the established tradition is that sweet foods are eaten at the end of a meal, as the desert, but in the ayurvedic understanding of digestion, it is better to eat the sweet food at the beginning of the meal, to kick off the digestive process in the mouth. Too much of the sweet taste at the end of a meal can slow down the digestive process.

# CHAPTER TWO

# Ayurveda
and the
mind

Another important aspect within ayurveda are the trigunas or three gunas (qualities), which are the three components or energies that make up the mind, known as 'sattva', 'rajas' and 'tamas'. As with the doshas, the balance between these is important in ayurvedic medicine and doctors will describe a patient's psychological constitution or 'manasa prakriti' based on the combination of these three gunas.

Everyone's psyche has a combination of the three gunas but the predominant one will determine a person's overall manasa prakriti.

**The sattva guna is linked to clarity and clear-mindedness.** It includes qualities such as harmony, truth, light, consciousness, an upward flow of energy, knowledge and happiness. When the mind is pure it can lead to self-realisation and enlightenment, unifying the mind and the heart.

**The rajas is the most active guna** and literally means smoke or stain, related to a distracted mind that looks outwards for stimulation and loses itself in the outside world. Its qualities include passion and high energy, movement, craving and desire. This mind has motion at its core and is driven by desires. It is linked to manipulation, willfulness, anger and ego plus the desire for power.

**The tamas guna is linked with lethargy and heaviness,** with traits such as delusion, laziness and apathy resulting from it, as well as qualities such as darkness, sloth, ignorance, obstruction and a downward flow of energy. The tamas mind may be dominated by external or subconscious forces, creating a servile nature.

In many cases rajas and tamas will exist together to some extent in a person's psyche, with rajas creating the energy and vitality and tamas grounding this energy and creating some stability.

People who know about the gunas will often joke that they are feeling 'tamasic' if they are feeling low on energy and slothful, or 'rajasic' if they are upbeat and full of energy. Most people will desire to have a sattvic lifestyle, with the clarity and peace of mind that goes with this, as well as the greatest freedom from disease.

# What is my triguna, mental type?

This chart may help you to see which is your predominant guna. Most people will have qualities that apply to all the gunas but you should find that one type is stronger. A better understanding of your own mental type will enable you to reduce the extremes that can become negative qualities if they exist in excess.

So, for instance, if you have a rajasic nature, being restless and agitated most of the time, this can lead to anxiety which could then also stimulate diseases that are related to stress. To help with this, you may need to look at ways to become more tamasic in your outlook, perhaps using meditation to calm you down.

Using the chart below, decide if you are sattvic, rajasic or tamasic for each of the categories, then mark your type for each category. In some categories you may feel that you comply to more than one guna so select two or more if this is the case.

At the end, add up all your scores to find out which is your predominant guna or what combination of the trigunas you have.

| Category | Sattvic |
|----------|---------|
| Romantic nature | Very romantic, caring and loyal |
| Sex drive | Can be quite low, more focused on love and cuddles |
| Addictive nature | Rarely get addicted to anything and find it easy to quit |
| Anger levels | Very rarely get angry, good at keeping calm |
| Coping with crisis | Cope very well, looking for the best, positive outcome |
| Leadership skills | A good leader, listen to others and make good decisions |
| Social interaction | Enjoy social interaction and have many friends |
| Communication | A good communicator and a good listener |

| Rajasic | Tamasik | score (S, R, T) |
|---------|---------|-----------------|
| Restless and controlling, not very empathetic | Can be vindictive and destructive, plus a bit needy | |
| Sometimes erratic but reasonable sex drive | High sex drive, may enjoy sexual exploration | |
| Can become addicted but self-love leads to quitting | Find it easy to become addicted and hard to give up | |
| Sometimes get angry, after provocation | Frequently get angry and frustrated | |
| Can become very agitated and cope badly with crisis | Run away from problems and hide under a stone | |
| Ambitious, controlling and like to dominate others | A bad leader, prefer to follow others or work alone | |
| Can be too self-focused and seen as fake by others | Fewer friends, but can be a stable and loyal friend | |
| Talk too quickly and not good at listening to others | Slightly fearful of communication, especially with strangers | |

| Category | Sattvic |
|---|---|
| Attitudes to rules and laws | Happy to follow the rules, unless they are obviously wrong |
| Learning ability | Enjoy learning new things and passing on information |
| Sleeping | Like a reasonable amount of sleep |
| Outlook | Fairly content and enjoy life with a positive outlook |
| Forgiving nature | Find it easy to forgive others and get on with life |
| Finances | Have a balanced outlook, enjoy both saving and spending |
| Attitude to work | Have a balanced attitude between work and social life |
| Sporting nature | Enjoy a wide range of sporting activities |

| Rajasic | Tamasik | score (S, R, T) |
|---|---|---|
| Can sometimes break the rules impulsively when it suits | Can break rules and drift into criminal pursuits if not careful | |
| Agitated mind, indecisive and not good at learning | Slow to learn and don't like new challenges | |
| Find it hard to relax and sleep | Like over-sleeping and inactivity | |
| Can swing between positive and negative outlook | Often have a dark, serious outlook | |
| Find it harder to forgive, like to see contrition in others | Rarely forgive, usually hold onto grudges for a long while | |
| Like to spend money and have the latest consumer goods | Hold onto money and possessions, don't like spending | |
| Work hard and fast, sometimes too focused on work | Like slow, plodding work with few challenges | |
| Into extreme sports and over exercising | Not into sports or team games | |

| Category | Sattvic |
|----------|---------|
| Violent nature | Rarely violent, always stay calm |
| Willpower | Strong willpower in most situations |
| Cleanliness | Like to be very clean and well-presented |
| Diet | Enjoy eating a balanced diet, prefer vegetarian food |

## HOW DO THE DOSHAS RELATE TO THE TRIGUNAS?

Ayurvedic doctors will consider a patient's dosha constitution as well as their triguna mental constitution, when prescribing treatment. The overall aim will be to better balance both the doshas and the trigunas.

A patient's triguna make-up could be made more extreme, depending on their dosha make-up. So, for instance a kapha

| Rajasic | Tamasik | score (S, R, T) |
|---|---|---|
| Can be violent if pushed and in a stressful situation | Often use violence if feeling stressed | |
| Willpower can slip sometimes | Very little willpower | |
| Prefer to be clean but not overtly worried | Not too bothered about cleanliness | |
| Crave stimulants and spicy foods | A large appetite and enjoy junk foods | |
| | **Final Total** | |

dosha patient, who has the tiredness and lethargy associated with this, could be even more slothful and lethargic if they are also tamasic. They would benefit greatly if they could change their mental attitude and become more sattvic, turning some of their negative qualities into more positive ones. Ultimately, bringing a person closer to the sattvic state will greatly help with their overall health, no matter what their dosha is.

A variety of treatments can be used to balance a patient's

triguna make-up. Meditation is considered the best medicine for the mind and, along with treatments such as yoga could, for instance, be used to make someone who is rajasic into someone who is calmer and more sattvic.

Even a change in diet regime could have an effect on someone's triguna state. Someone who is too rajasic may benefit by reducing dietary stimulants such as coffee, for instance.

The environment we live and work in is also important, so someone who is rajasic and who works in an extremely stressful job might benefit from a move to less stressful environment, or from allocating some time out from their working day for meditation.

# CHAPTER THREE

# Ayurvedic therapies

I n ayurveda there are a wide variety of different therapies that can be used, from diet and herbal medication to things such as cleansing the intestine with the use of enemas, as well as the use of meditation or massages.

Most of these therapies can fit under the two headings of 'tonification' or 'reduction'. Tonification therapies are those which are designed to increase or supplement while reduction therapies are designed to decrease excesses within the body.

With most illnesses, a reduction therapy will be recommended first, since this is designed to remove toxins and can reduce the doshas that have become too high and aggravated. For instance, a person with an excess of kapha dosha, who has become overweight and has health problems because of this, may be recommended a diet regime that has a reduction nature.

After a reduction therapy has been used, then often a ton-ification therapy may be used to build the body back up again afterwards. So, if a patient has undergone an intense reduction process to treat a particular illness, then tonification can be used to rebuild their constitution afterwards.

In particular, vata types may need tonification therapy more than others because they are often under-weight and illnesses may stem from this, in the same way that kapha types can become ill due to being overweight.

When related purely to body size, this is an area where Western medicine and ayurveda probably share the most common ground, with most people being well aware of the problems of being obese and having to eat more healthily, though often much less is said about the underweight people who struggle to build body mass, since being thin is the most desired body shape in modern culture.

Until fairly recently, this was not so true in India, where a larger body shape was often seen as more desirable, partly because it pointed to a wealthy lifestyle. Today, though, Western influences have penetrated Indian culture to the point where being slim is now often seen as the more desirable body shape.

## TONIFICATION THERAPIES

In ayurveda, tonification therapies are those which build-up the body and they can be used on their own, or after a reduction therapy to help the patient recover.

Patients who are underweight or elderly, or have suffered

from a debilitating disease, may be recommended tonification therapy to build them back up. These illnesses are often seen as vata in nature and people with the vata dosha are more likely to need tonification therapies.

Tonification therapies often involve the diet, with rich foods that help to build-up the body. They can include dairy products, sweet foods like honey as well as nuts and seeds. Lifestyle changes may also be recommended, such as taking more sleep or getting a better work/life balance.

Other tonification therapies include enemas, done with a special mixture of herbs, oil and water, and which are designed to rehydrate the intestine as much as cleanse it.

Special oils, sometimes with herbs added, can also be used in tonification, either applied to the skin or taken internally. They can also be applied through the nose, which is seen as a way of nourishing the brain.

## REDUCTION THERAPIES

Generally, most types of reduction therapy will be harder for a patient to undertake than tonification therapies, since they normally involve cutting back on foods or other things we enjoy or have become used to, or even addicted to. For many people this change is tough, with therapies such as fasting or even the use of vomiting or enemas being quite hard to take.

Reduction therapies fall into two types, palliation and purification. A palliation therapy is one that is designed to calm the body and remove the undigested ama food waste which has accumulated and which is toxic for the body. A typical palliation therapy in ayurveda may include fasting or taking a special herb mixture or diet that will increase the digestive fire (agni) and help to remove the ama toxic waste.

The purification therapies can be a bit tougher and are designed to fully cleanse the body and balance the doshas. There are five types of purification therapy, known as 'pancha karma' and these are carried out in a clinic by an ayurvedic doctor and I will now explain them in more detail.

# Pancha karma

The concept of 'detox' has become increasingly popular in recent years, when it comes to diet or even giving up alcohol for a period of time. It is another area where ayurvedic thinking has been way ahead of modern thinking, with a variety of what could be called detox treatments forming a core of ayurvedic medicine.

The most prominent of these is used in reduction therapy and is known as pancha karma, with 'pancha' translating as 'five' and 'karma' translating as 'actions'. The pancha karma program is a five-stage body cleansing or detoxification process that is designed to restore the digestive system and the digestive fire (agni) and balance the doshas.

If the five doshas are out of balance, agni can be reduced and this results in a build-up of toxic waste in the body, known as ama. If this is only in fairly limited quantities, then an ayurvedic doctor might just use palliation and recommend a cleansing diet, one that will remove the sort of oily, sweet and heavy foods normally associated with increasing the kapha dosha and which can slow down the agni.

If the agni is really low in a patient, with a large build-up of ama, this can also affect other parts of the body such as the circulatory system and can also reduce the strength of the immune system. In this case, an ayurvedic doctor may recommend pancha karma as the best treatment. This can be a fairly extreme course of treatment and is normally only carried out in an ayurvedic clinic, under the supervision of a doctor.

The five processes used in pancha karma therapy are therapeutic vomiting (vamana), purgation (virechana), enemas (basti), nasal application of herbs and oils (nasya) and blood-letting (rakta moksha).

In preparation for pancha karma, a patient normally spends a week or more on a special diet that will remove stimulants such as coffee and alcohol and will normally involve a very basic vegetarian regime. This can be a tough week for anyone addicted to stimulants such as caffeine, possibly causing big headaches, but by the end of the week the patient should be feeling refreshed and ready for the pancha karma treatment.

## THE TREATMENT PROCESS

An ayurvedic doctor will assess a patient's needs during the treatment process and will decide which of the five processes to use and in some cases may use all of them. A patient could stay in the clinic for a week or more, undergoing the treatments, before going home and adapting back to normal life over a week or so, following a diet regime set out by the doctor. So, it's a time-consuming process and can be relatively expensive, especially for poorer Indian people, but it's a popular treatment, even carried out by some tourists who visit India specifically for this.

## VAMANA

Looking at the five processes individually, the vomiting (vamana) treatment is one that may now be frowned upon in Western culture, due to its association with illnesses such as bulimia and anorexia, but in ayurveda it is seen as a way of cleaning the stomach and removing the toxic waste or ama that has built up in parts of the stomach. This liquid waste is viewed in terms of the kapha dosha, so releasing it will reduce excess kapha in the body.

An ayurvedic doctor will stimulate vomiting either with strong herbal teas or perhaps just salty water and it is important that the stomach is fully emptied.

This treatment will not be recommended for all, and usually not for anyone who is too old or emaciated. Following the treatment, an anti-kapha diet will normally be recommended, to stop the future build-up of ama toxins.

## VIRECHANA

The purgation or virechana process is seen as one of the easiest to administer and it's something that even Western medicine relies on occasionally. For, instance the use of an endoscope will often require the digestive system to be emptied beforehand.

In ayurvedic medicine, purgation is stimulated by natural products such as caster oil or even rhubarb root. If these are taken one day, the purgation should start the next day, with frequent visits to the toilet required, until the digestive system is fully emptied.

Purgation is a way of removing waste products in the small intestine, which is seen in terms of the pitta dosha. So, removing this waste will remove excess pitta from the body. It is useful for treating problems such as diarrhea, constipation or food poisoning.

## BASTI

The use of enemas as part of the pancha karma process is seen as a way of removing toxic waste products that have built up in the colon. This is a part of the body associated with the vata dosha, so removing waste here will remove excess vata.

An enema is usually given with a liquid that is warm water with salt added, as well as a mixture of herbs and something like sesame oil. These extra ingredients are added to make the enema less harsh and stop it from drying out or irritating the colon.

## NASYA

The nasya or nasal cleaning process in ayurveda is where a mixture of herbs is given via the nose either as a snuff-type powder or as a herbal oil. It is designed to cleanse, nourish and decongest the nasal cavity and is mainly seen as helping to reduce kapha and vata dosha-related conditions or illnesses.

Different ayurvedic doctors may have their own preparations for use in nasya therapy, often with different mixtures to deal with the different dosha types, or to deal with different types of illness.

## RAKTA MOKSHA

The rakta moksha or blood-letting therapy is one that has long been used in ayurvedic medicine and was also popular in Western medicine until not that long ago. It is now used less frequently even in ayurvedic treatments and is not as drastic as it might sound.

An ayurvedic doctor will only remove very small amounts of blood, from specific parts of the body, usually on the back. The blood taken from these specific sites is seen as toxic, so removing it allows it to be replaced by new, clean blood.

As an alternative to blood-letting, an ayurvedic doctor might instead recommend a treatment that contains blood-cleansing herbs, which the patient can take orally over an extended period of time.

## AFTER PANCHA KARMA

Once pancha karma has taken place, and the patient has returned to normal life, follow-up treatments may be recommended and even another session of pancha karma may be needed, but usually not sooner than a month or more after the initial treatment.

The patient will be recommended a diet that is better for their particular dosha constitution, so that the build-up of ama waste is reduced in the future. This will typically be low on dairy, meat and very sweet foods but with lots of vegetables and helpful spices.

As I mentioned in the introduction to the book, I have undertaken pancha karma myself, under the supervision of my ayurvedic doctor in Varanasi in India. It was a tough process, taking 20 days in total, but I felt totally rejuvenated afterwards and, if my doctor thinks it is a good idea, I plan to do it again when I am next back in India.

# Oil and herb therapy

The use of oils is an important part of ayurvedic treatment, with some often used as part of the pancha karma treatment. Among a wide range of applications, they can be applied to the skin, into the nasal cavity, into the mouth or ears, or be used as part of an enema mixture.

Oils are often mixed with herbs to treat different conditions and different types of oil are used for the three dosha types, normally to lower some of the extremes associated with that particular dosha.

So, for instance, for those with vata dosha, sesame oil is often used as its warm nature balances the cold nature of vata. It is an oil that absorbs really easily into the skin and can be mixed with various natural herbs to make oils that can help with a variety of vata illnesses, though it is also used to treat the other doshas as well.

For those with a kapha dosha, lighter oils tend to be used as a base for treatments, to counter the heavy nature of kapha. These can include flaxseed oil (or linseed oil), as well as sunflower oil, plus sesame oil can also be used. These oils can be mixed with herbs or essential oils, such as pine and sage oil, and kapha oil treatments may be stimulating rather than calming, to counteract the heavy nature of kapha.

With the pitta dosha, cooling and calming oil treatments are often used, to counteract the fiery nature of this dosha type. Coconut oil is often used as a base for pitta preparations, plus sunflower oil and ghee (clarified butter) can also be used. They are often mixed with herbs that also have a cool and calming effect when treating pitta conditions.

An ayurvedic doctor will have a wide range of prepared oils that can be used in therapy and, during a consultation, can recommend the best type for each patient, as well as saying how they should be applied.

As a starting point, you could always begin to use one of the oils recommended for your dosha type as a general skin lubricant or moisturizer. Coconut oil, in particular, can be good for soothing and softening the skin and also has some anti-bacterial qualities that can help to clear up minor skin conditions.

## HERBS USED IN THERAPY

A huge range of natural herbs and spices are used in ayurvedic therapy and can be taken on their own or as part of a mixture designed to treat a particular condition. They are normally either taken as a powder, mixed with water (often mixed together when the water is hot) or mixed with oils so that they can be applied externally or sometimes ingested.

They may also be mixed and ingested with foodstuffs that are appropriate for a particular dosha type. So, warm milk can be used for vata types, ghee for pitta types and honey for kapha types.

Your ayurvedic doctor will prescribe and normally supply you with the herbal preparation that will treat your particular illnesses, taking into account your dosha type.

## EXAMPLES OF HERBAL PREPARATIONS

I will give a few examples of some simple ayurvedic herbal preparations here, to give you an idea of the different types of formulation. If you have specific health issues, I would always recommend talking to your ayurveda doctor, or allopathic doctor, before taking any herbal remedies. Sometimes the ingredients may clash with, or reduce the effectiveness of, other medication you may be taking.

**Used as a sedative and tonic for calming the nerves**, ashwagandha is mixed with ghee (clarified butter), with a small amount then taken daily, mixed with milk. The herb ashwagandha is now easily available outside India and many people take it as an anti-cancer supplement or even as an aphrodisiac.

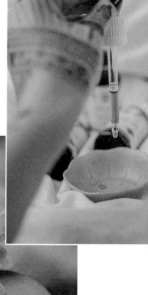

Personally, I take ashwagandha every morning, mixed in with a fresh, green fruit juice, to help put me in a good mood for the day.

**Used as a way of stimulating digestion**, coriander is mixed in equal parts with dry ginger, black pepper, Indian long pepper (pippali), nutmeg and cloves. This fiery formula may be too stimulating for pitta dosha types, but can help to reduce the excesses of the kapha dosha and help with the slow digestion often common to kapha types.

**Used as a laxative to help with constipation or aid weight loss**, dry ginger is mixed with bayberry (wax myrtle) and prickly ash, with a small amount taken before meals, mixed with honey or warm water. This type of weight-loss formula is often recommended for kapha dosha types. It's also interesting to note that all the individual ingredients used are recognized individually for their health benefits, with the small berries of the prickly ash tree used for helping with joint pain and circulation problems, plus some people also take it for its anti-cancer properties. Likewise, ginger is also often taken by many for its anti-oxidant, cancer-preventing properties.

**Used as a blood purification tonic**, lemongrass, barberry, dry ginger, sandalwood and vetiver root are mixed together, with one part individually of ginger and lemon grass, mixed with two parts individually of all the other ingredients. This can be taken as a powder, or as tablets, with warm water, ghee or honey. As well as cleansing the blood, it can help with fevers, burns and headaches. A fairly light, vegetarian diet should be observed while taking the tonic, to help in its effectiveness.

# Gem therapy

To the modern, scientific mind, the use of gems might seem ephemeral, materialistic and not directly related to health, but in ayurvedic thinking they have real importance.

Gem therapy evolved from a time when ayurveda and astrology were closely linked in ancient vedic thinking. Different gem stones are associated with different planets and can be used to alter the effects that a particular planet may have on a person, according to their star sign or more specifically their vedic birth chart.

Gems are mainly used to help the mind and with 'prana', which is the universal energy that flows through us and around us.

It's very rare that ayurvedic gem therapy will actually involve the ingestion of a ground-up gem stone, though sometimes stones are soaked in alcohol or other liquids for a period of time to create a tincture which can then be taken.

In most cases, gem therapy involves wearing the gem stone as a ring or necklace. Where a particular gem stone is very expensive, it's often possible to get similar benefits with an alternative, cheaper stone, so you don't have to be rich to partake in gem therapy.

The metal used to mount the gem is important, with gold seen as having a warming effect and silver a colder effect. In addition, the gem should also be in contact with the skin to have the maximum effect, so a ring or locket will have to be designed with this in mind.

If you are interested in gem therapy, a good starting point is to have your birth chart produced by a professional vedic astrologer, so that they can then recommend gem stones that may help balance the influence of the planets on you.

I'll include here some information about a few key gem stones that are used in ayurvedic healing, so you can see how this therapy works and apply it to yourself.

## BENEFITS OF DIFFERENT GEMS
### Pearl or mukta

Taken from a sea oyster, pearls are a refined form of calcium and have a cold, watery energy. Because of this they can increase kapha and decrease pitta and vata. They are also associated with Shiva, the Hindu god, because he also originally came out of the water, namely from the water of the sacred Ganges River.

Pearls can have a calming effect with mental and emotional problems, helping with insomnia. They can also help boost the female reproductive system.

Pearls can be worn in many ways, but set in a silver mount and worn as a ring is a common way of wearing them in India.

### Ruby or manakya

The red ruby stone is seen as having a hot nature. Because of this, it can help reduce kapha and vata but increases pitta.

Ruby is used in ayurveda to help build up the heart as well as helping with circulation and digestion. It may also help with depression and anxiety.

Ruby gems will normally be set in gold and worn as a ring.

### Red coral or praval

Formed in the sea by a special type of worm, red coral has a pale rose-red colour and has a warm energy, combining water and fire. It can increase kapha and reduce vata, having a more neutral effect on pitta.

It is used in ayurveda to help with diseases of the heart, strengthening the blood system and improving energy levels. It is sometimes also seen as an aphrodisiac and also has an anti-toxic nature that can help cure fevers.

Red coral is usually worn on a ring and set in silver.

## Emerald or panna

The emerald is a green-coloured, transparent gem stone which has a slightly cool, watery energy. It increases kapha and reduces pitta, while having a more neutral effect on vata.

It can help with poisoning of the body and liver problems as well as calming and regulating the nervous system, reducing pain. It is also said to be good to help with degenerative diseases such as cancer.

The emerald is normally worn as a ring and set in gold, though hot pitta types may use cooler silver instead.

## Diamond or heera

The diamond gem is a pure form of carbon and has a slightly cool water and air energy. It increases kapha but decreases pitta and vata.

It can help with problems of the kidneys and is said to help generally with chronic ailments. Zircon can have similar effect, for those who can't afford diamonds.

Diamonds are normally worn as a ring and set in white gold.

## Blue sapphire or neelam

The blue sapphire is, as its name suggests, blue in colour. It has a cold, air nature and decreases kapha and pitta but increases vata.

It can help to keep negative energies at bay and helps to calm emotions and nerve problems, leading to a feeling of well-being.

Blue sapphire is normally worn as a ring, set in gold to warm it up a bit, though hot pitta types may opt for silver instead.

## Cat's eye or vaidurya

The cat's eye gem is a blue-coloured stone with streaks of white and has a hot air and fire nature. As such, it increases pitta but reduces kapha and vata.

It is seen as a stimulating gem that can help increase mental and spiritual powers. It is often the stone chosen by astrologers for themselves, to enhance their perception.

It can be worn as a necklace or as a ring, where it is often mounted in silver.

## Quartz crystal or sphatic

Quartz can come in a variety of different colours and clear quartz is often used in ayurvedic therapy. It is seen as a stone that can amplify the influences around it, increasing the good or sometimes the bad.

It is connected with purity of mind and awareness and can

be used to balance the chakra (energy centres) within the body as well as helping to balance all the doshas.

It can be worn as a ring, often mounted in silver, or as a necklace or on many other parts of the body.

## CHOOSING A GEM

In ayurvedic gem therapy, it is important that the gem stone be pure, so if it's a clear type of gem it should have no opacity or internal spots or cracks. It should also have a uniform colour and not be a mixture of different colours or markings. Something like cat's eye is an exception here, with its white streak being part of its nature.

It's worth doing more research and also

checking with a vedic astrologer before choosing gem stones, especially if they are really expensive ones.

From a personal perspective, I spoke to my ayurvedic doctor many years ago when I was having stomach problems and, after a long consultation, he gave me a stone to wear. He told me to have the stone set in silver and worn as a ring.

I later discovered this stone was hessonite, which in ayurveda is used for increasing feelings of self-respect and self-love, as well as for increasing intuition and helping with the 'third eye chakra' energy center. It also helps to draw off negative influences that can cause ill health.

My doctor later explained that he had recommended this stone to help with my mind, making me calmer and more self-respecting, which in turn would help with my stomach problems.

Wearing the stone, I did feel calmer and my stomach problems gradually went away. So, since then, I have become much more interested in gem stones and gem therapy. I now use gems in various ways, including placing them throughout my house to help with energy flows.

# Meditation Therapy

In ayurvedic thinking, the mind, spirit and body are all very much connected, so therapies that deal with the mind can also help with health issues. These therapies include meditation, the repeating of mantras and also prayer.

Meditation is either used on its own, or as a way of increasing the power of another treatment, such as a herbal preparation. This might take the form of a ritual used in the preparation of the herbal medicine, which involves meditation to increase the potency of the medicine. The meditation might also be directed at a particular divine power, or god, so that this energy also goes towards making the medicine effective.

Meditation can also be used on its own as part of a treatment, where it can help with stress-related illnesses and even ailments such as heart problems, where a calming period of meditation can relieve stress on the heart and help it to heal.

Meditation can be particularly useful for

diseases related to the nervous system such as insomnia or regular headaches and may be used alongside herbal remedies or diet regimes. Diseases of the nervous system are seen as vata dosha illnesses, so therapies to help will generally have an anti-vata nature, to reduce excess vata.

Many people in Western culture have pre-conceived ideas about meditation, perhaps being scared that it will empty their mind and leave more space for bad thoughts. Actually, though, proper meditation is about calming the mind and bringing peace and tranquility, not emptying it, so there is nothing to fear. Meditation also helps us to live in the present, right here, right now, and not to dwell on the past or worry about the future.

Learning to do it properly can take time, especially with those who live busy lives and are focused heavily on the fast-paced, materialistic nature of the modern world.

Personally, I use meditation to help calm me down when I am anxious as well as for clearing my mind from daily worries. Meditation has helped train my mind to become more self-caring, self-loving and to be able to share more and help others.

When suffering from illnesses I have also used meditation to observe my fears and anxieties as well as any pain. Meditation techniques such as visualization or mantra repetition can change your view of how you see and experience pain, which reduces the fear of pain. For instance, meditating on a beautiful image in your mind can reduce anxiety and pain.

This use of meditation in healing is another area where ancient ayurvedic thinking is being reflected in modern holistic health treatments and it can be a very powerful tool.

# Mantra Therapy

Often used as part of meditation, mantras also have a part to play in ayurvedic therapies, where they are seen as divine sounds and energies, that can aid healing on a spiritual level.

The word 'mantra' has an interesting background. The 'man' part of the word comes from the ancient Sanskrit 'man' which is used as a stem in other words and roughly translates as 'to think'. It forms the stem of the word 'manushya' which is the Sanskrit word for human being or man, which can also be translated as a 'thinking being'.

In ancient Sanskrit, the creator of the world, the 'God', is called 'Manu' and 'manushya' also means the 'child of Manu'. The English words 'man', 'mental' and 'mind' have evolved from the Greek word 'menos', which itself evolved from the Sanskrit word root 'man'. The word 'mantra' also developed from the same root, so it relates back to the idea of humans as thinking beings and has developed to mean a certain word which, when used in repetition, can have a strong effect on the human mind.

As a rough translation, the 'man' part of mantra means 'mind' while the 'tra' part translates as 'transport'. So, a mantra is something that can be used to transport the mind, often taking you into a meditative state. In ancient Sanskrit terms, it could be seen as a tool that helps purify the mind of the manushya (human) so that they can connect more with Manu, the original creative force. This accords with the likes of Buddhist thinking, where meditation is a tool used to help achieve enlightenment.

As with meditation in general, mantras in ayurveda can either be used directly to help with physical and mental health problems, or can be used to energize herbal preparations or specific diet foods.

The power of a mantra comes with repetition and a particular mantra may need to be repeated many thousands of times for it to have an effect on the mind and the subconscious. It can either be sung out loudly, muttered quietly or even take the form of a silent thought. The repetition of a mantra is known as 'japa' in Sanskrit.

Sometimes, the transmission of a special mantra word from a guru to a disciple is used as part of a religious initiation, with that mantra then remaining secret and used in meditation.

## MANTRAS USED IN AYURVEDIC HEALING

For those wanting to use mantras and meditation as a healing process, it is best to find an experienced teacher to act as your guide and guru. They will be able to help you find the best

mantra for you, with different mantras seen as having different healing properties in ayurveda.

The most powerful mantras can be a single word, repeated over and over, but longer mantras have also evolved and have specific names, such as the Gayatri Mantra and Dhanvantra Mantra. These longer mantras often refer to a god, asking for help from that particular god. To give you an example, here are the Sanskrit words of the Gayatri Mantra:

Om Bhur Bhuvah Svah

Tat Savitur Varanyam

Bhargo Devasya Dheemahi

Dhiyo Yo Nah Prachodayat

This mantra is a praise to the word 'Om' which is the quiet, humming sound of the universe, with the hope that concentrating on it may help to enlighten us. Om is the primordial sound and is the word most often used in mantras. The Gayatri Mantra is seen as one of the most powerful healing mantras and opens the doors of perception, making us more aware, conscious and tuned into ourselves.

Its healing properties come from purifying our minds, helping both our mental and by extension our physical health.

## HEALING MANTRA WORDS

Some of the single mantra words are linked with specific types of healing in ayurveda. They can be very powerful and need to be repeated continually, often for thousands of times. They often form part of more complex mantras, with Om in particular being common in longer mantras.

I will list a few of the main mantra words here, to give you an idea of how they are seen as having different healing properties.

## Om

As used in the Gayatri Mantra, Om is the most important mantra, seen as a link to the energy that powers the universe. As such it forms the beginning and end of many longer mantras and is seen as clearing the mind and increasing perception.

## AIM (pronounced aym)

This is seen as a good mantra to help with the mind and mental health and can be used in ayurveda to help with nervous disorders.

### HRIM (pronounced hreem)

This mantra helps with purification, related to the mind but also helpful during detoxification regimes.

### HUM (pronounced with a soft 'u')

This mantra can help to remove bad influences and negative emotions, also helping to remove external factors that may cause disease

### SHAM (pronounced more like shum)

This mantra is used to promote calmness and contentment and can help calm the mind for people with mental health problems.

# Massage Therapy

A s with other therapies in ayurveda, massages are used to balance the doshas, either reducing an excess of one or increasing those that are lacking. Different dosha types benefit from different types of massage, ranging from a heavy deep-tissue massage to a light facial massage. Also, concentrating the massage on a particular part of the body, related to a particular dosha, can also have an impact on that dosha.

In addition, special ayurvedic oils are normally used during a massage, normally herbal oils which are specifically formulated for a particular dosha type.

I'll give a run-down here of how massage can benefit each dosha. Again, though, I would recommend seeking out an ayurvedic doctor or ayurveda massage specialist to find out which treatment is best for you.

## VATA MASSAGES

As the cold, dry, airy dosha, vata is best treated with a massage that adds warmth, moisture and which helps to ground the airy excesses of Vata. An excess of the vata dosha can make someone anxious, often leading to a lack of appetite and conditions such as insomnia. So, a massage which concentrates on vata should help with conditions such as these.

## PITTA MASSAGES

As the hot, light dosha, pitta is best treated with calming and cooling massages, paying attention to pitta areas such as the stomach. An excess of the pitta dosha can led to irritability, temper, constant thirst and stomach problems, all of which should be helped by a pitta-focused massage treatment.

## KAPHA MASSAGES

As the heavy and watery dosha, kapha is best treated with massages that stimulate the body, such as a deep-tissue massage. An excess of the kapha dosha can lead to lethargy, depression, obesity and a general lack of energy and drive. A good kapha-focused massage should help to energize a patient and set them on a more dynamic, healthier path.

## TYPES OF AYURVEDIC MASSAGE

There is, of course, a massive range of different types of massage and, when you add in the herbal oils that can also be added to treat each dosha type, you can see that care needs to be taken in choosing the right massage treatment.

I'll list a few of the types used in ayurveda here. They are normally given Sanskrit names that relate to the type of massage or the area treated.

### Shirodhara massage

This type of massage concentrates on the 'third eye chakra', with soothing oils poured over the forehead and gently massaged-in. This massage has a calming effect on the nervous system, making people feel calmer and more aware. It can be particularly good for vata dosha types, helping to ground them.

## Marma abhyanga massage

This type of full body massage applies pressure and friction to the 'marma' points which are the vital energy junctions in the body. Stimulating them creates a healthier energy flow in the body and can help with detoxification as well as helping with stress and aiding relaxation. This type of massage can be particularly good for pitta dosha types, helping them to calm down.

## Gandharva massage

This is a type of massage that uses sound energy from singing bowls, along with herbal oils, for a massage to stimulate all the senses and revitalize. It can be good for all of the dosha types, being both calming as well as stimulating the senses.

## Udvartana massage

This type of massage uses cleansing herbal oils which are massaged into the body, to help reduce water retention and also to help detoxify the skin. The water-reducing nature of this massage makes it particularly good for kapha dosha types.

# CHAPTER FOUR

# Ayurveda
# and Yoga

Both an important part of the ancient vedic texts, yoga and ayurveda developed alongside each other and, while many people in the West just think about yoga in terms of the physical asanas (yoga postures) which may form the majority of a yoga class, it is a complete way of living which also includes aspects such as meditation and use of mantras, which are also used as treatments in ayurveda.

Another important therapy shared by both ayurveda and yoga is that of 'pranayama', which is a form of controlled breathing. About 25 years ago I asked an experienced yogin what he thought the most important components of yoga were and he explained that only about 20% of yoga relates to the postures (asanas), with 30% about breathing (pranayama) and 50% concentrating on meditation. So, in his view, pranayama is more important than the asanas, which most people normally see as the main part of yoga.

Breathing is perhaps an aspect of health that is often overlooked but the intake of air is obviously as important as the intake of food when it comes to life and health.

The breathing exercises that make up pranayama are designed to help the flow of energy in the body, which in turn brings general health benefits. Pranayama exercises work by regulating the inhalation of breath, the retention of breath

and the exhalation of breath, as well as regulating how deep or shallow each breath is.

Pranayama exercises are sometimes done as part of a yoga class and there are different forms of pranayama. A common method, called 'nadi shodhana' (alternate nostril breathing), is where a finger is used to hold one nostril closed during breathing, then this is alternated to close the other nostril. The length of each breath is also regulated, with students perhaps asked to count to ten during inhalation, hold their breath for another count of ten, the release their breath slowly over another counted time period.

Another form of pranayama is 'kapalabhati' (skull shining breath) where breathing is done to a fast rhythm, with strong abdominal force used to expel each breath. This is seen as detoxifying and invigorating for the body.

Pranayama is something you can also practice outside a yoga class, perhaps for 20 minutes or so each day to make you feel more active and alert. However, the types of pranayama that involve very fast rhythms of breathing are not recommended for those that suffer from some medical conditions such as asthma, or heart problems or for women who are pregnant. It can also make you feel a bit dizzy and light-headed if you are not used to it.

# Ayurveda and the Seven Chakras

I have already talked about how ayurveda views the body as having many energy flows which, when blocked, can lead to disease. The various energy centres in the body are referred to as chakras. There are many chakras, but the main ones are referred to as the 'seven chakras'.

They control everything from your health to your mental wellbeing, moods and spirituality. The seven chakras are as follows:

Crown chakra (sahasrara)

Third-Eye chakra (ajna)

Throat chakra (vishuddha)

Heart chakra (anahata)

Solar-plexus chakra (manipura)

Sacral chakra (swadhisthana)

Root chakra (muladara)

These are listed above in the descending order in which they occur in the body, starting with the crown chakra in the head down to the root chakra at the base of the spine.

Energy within the body travels within the chakras and between them and illness can occur when the chakras are blocked, or when they are underactive or overactive. Chakra healing will often aim to balance the chakras, in the same way that other types of ayurvedic healing will seek to balance the doshas.

Ayurvedic treatments often use certain herbal remedies to align the chakras and treat imbalances. Ginger, black pepper, ashwagandha and turmeric are just a few examples of the herbs and spices used in chakra therapy. Yoga and other therapies can also be used to treat the chakras.

Each chakra also has characteristics such its own colour and shape, accorded to it by ancient sages. Each also has associated gem stones which are seen as balancing that particular chakra.

**The root chakra** has dark red colour and is associated with agate, hematite and blood stone. It is located at the base of the spine is associated with the vata dosha and when this chakra is open we feel confident and active but when it is blocked we can feel insecure. Yoga and herbal remedies can be used as a therapy to help here.

**The sacral chakra** has a yellow colour and is linked with citrine, moonstone and coral. It is associated with vata and pitta doshas and is located in the lower abdomen. If this chakra is open we feel creative and balanced, but if it is blocked we can feel that we lack control of our lives. Again, yoga can be a useful therapy to help with this chakra.

**The solar plexus chakra** has an orange colour and linked to citrine, malachite and topaz. It is located in the upper abdomen area and is associated with the pitta dosha. If it is open, we feel emotionally stable but we feel more unstable if it is blocked.

Pranayama breathing therapy, as well as herbal preparations, can help with this chakra.

**The heart chakra** has a green (or sometimes pink) colour and is linked to green calcite, rose quartz and green tourmaline. It

is located in the chest, with the heart, and is associated with all three doshas. If this chakra is open we feel love and compassion, with these feelings affected if this chakra is blocked. Massages with oils and various herbal treatments can be used to treat the heart chakra.

**The throat chakra** has a blue colour and is linked with aquamarine, lapis lazuli and turquoise. It is associated with vata and kapha doshas and controls our ability to communicate, so a blockage means we find it harder to express ourselves. The chanting of mantras and herbal remedies are often used to treat this chakra.

**The third eye chakra** has a magenta/mauve colour and is linked to amethyst and black obsidian. It is located in the forehead and is associated with vata and pitta doshas. Blockages here can lead to headaches and problems with concentration. Meditation, pranayama and certain herbs can help here.

**The crown chakra** has a white, transparent, crystal clear colour and is linked to diamonds and clear quartz. It is located at the top of the head and is associated with the vata dosha. If this chakra is fully open it can lead to bliss and enlightenment, but if blocked it can lead to negative thoughts and cynicism. Meditation, silence and certain herb preparations can help with this chakra.

With most of the chakras, yoga, meditation and pranayama can have a positive effect and these are things you can practice quite easily at home or with a yoga teacher, to help open and align your chakras.

# CHAPTER 5

# Ayurvedic Diet and Recipes

Perhaps the easiest way to use ayurveda in your daily life is by observing an ayurvedic diet regime. As with all the other therapies, this is related back to the three doshas and certain foods will lower a particular dosha while others will increase it. A carefully planned diet which takes into account your dosha constitution and tries to create a better balance should lead to a healthy, long life, which is the ultimate goal in Ayurveda.

## FOOD QUALITIES

The qualities of individual foodstuffs are the key to planning an ayurvedic diet and there are several things to take into account.

One of these is the physical quality of the food, from whether it is hot or cold, to whether it is oily or dry, or if it is seen as heavy or light. So, for example, chili pepper is a hot food, whereas milk or the herb mint are seen as cold foods. Dairy and meat products can be heavy and slow when it comes to digestion but rice is seen as a light food.

If these food qualities match the qualities of a particular dosha, then they can increase the level of that dosha in a person when consumed. So, chili peppers can increase the fiery pitta dosha but a cool glass of milk will help reduce the pitta dosha. If you have kapha dosha, the heavy, slow foods such as meat will increase this, but light foods like rice or fiery foods like chili pepper will help reduce this. Vata is the dry, airy dosha, so heavy foods like cheese can help to reduce this, while hot, dry, light foods will increase it. So, for instance, some dry cereals can increase vata.

## THE SIX TASTES

I have mentioned the 'six tastes' earlier in the book and these are also very important when choosing food to increase or decrease a particular dosha.

The six tastes are sweet, sour, salty, pungent, bitter and astringent and each taste is made up of the five basic elements of fire, earth, water, air and ether. So, for instance, the salty taste is made up of water and fire, while the sour taste is made up of earth and fire.

These basic elements are also fundamental in each of the three doshas, with vata being the air dosha, pitta the fire dosha and kapha the water dosha. If you take a food that has the same quality as your particular dosha, it will increase the dosha. So, for instance, if a kapha dosha person eats a watery, heavy food, this will increase the level of the kapha dosha. Instead, a kapha dosha person should eat dry, airy foods, which will reduce any excess of the kapha dosha and therefore help reduce the health problems that come with having an excess of that dosha.

I'll add a small chart here so you can see how the different tastes affect each dosha.

| Taste | Vata | Pitta | Kapha |
|-------|------|-------|-------|
| Sweet | decreases | decreases | increases |
| Sour | decreases | increases | increases |
| Salty | decreases | increases | increases |
| Pungent | increases | increases | decreases |
| Bitter | increases | decreases | decreases |
| Astringent | increases | decreases | decreases |

Once you have worked out your own dosha make-up, you can then start planning a diet regime that takes account of this. Your aim should be to reduce your intake of foods that increase your dosha and increase intake of foods that reduce it. At the same time, you can also focus on the dosha or doshas you are most lacking, eating foods that will increase levels of these.

I will include a few simple recipes here, showing how each one will affect each dosha. After a while, you'll get an intuitive feel for which foods will be good for your particular dosha constitution and will take this into account when cooking.

I think it's also important to treat yourself, so if you're a kapha dosha type and really love sweet foods, why not treat yourself to a slice of cake every now and then? Your ayurvedic knowledge will tell you that you can always counteract this to an extent by then taking something astringent like a black tea.

## AYURVEDIC RECIPES

Enjoying an ayurvedic diet doesn't have to involve giving up meat or dairy products, though this is often part of some religions that have a base in ayurveda. For instance, Hindus don't eat the meat of the holy cow, so your burger in a Delhi take-way will likely be from lamb rather than beef.

Like myself, I am assuming most people who are interested in ayurveda outside India are probably going to be vegetarian, or vegan, for reasons of animal welfare, personal health, or even from an environmental perspective since meat farming does so much damage.

So, I will include a handful of vegetarian and vegan recipes here, to give you some inspiration for ayurvedic cooking.

# BLACK LENTIL DAL

One of the many thick-soup style dal dishes that form a staple diet for many people in India. Being heavy and spicy, it reduces vata, but increases pitta and kapha.

l cup of split black lentils
6 cups of water
2 chopped carrots
1 large, chopped onion
3 crushed garlic cloves
2 tablespoons of vegetable oil or ghee
l teaspoon of turmeric
1 teaspoon of dried cumin
1 teaspoon of salt
juice of one lemon
l tablespoon of grated ginger
l teaspoon of dried coriander (or use fresh leaves)
¼ teaspoon of chili or cayenne pepper

Put the lentils and water into a saucepan and bring to the boil, then cover and simmer for up to an hour, until the lentils are soft.

Meanwhile, put the oil or ghee into a frying pan and add the dried spices, cooking for a minute or so before adding the chopped onion and garlic and lemon juice. Fry on a gentle heat until the onions are soft and tender.

When the lentils are cooked and soft, add the fried ingredients to them in the saucepan, as well as the chopped carrots, ginger and salt. Cover the saucepan and cook for a further 20 minutes or so, adding more water if needed. It should end up as a thick soup and can be served on its own or with rice.

# PAN-FRIED OKRA

A soothing food that is good for digestion, reducing fiery pitta and also vata but increasing kapha.

½ kg fresh okra
3 tablespoons of vegetable oil or ghee
1 flat teaspoon of turmeric
½ teaspoon fenugreek seed
2 teaspoons of coriander powder
½ teaspoon ground cumin
¼ teaspoon black pepper
½ teaspoon salt

Wash and dry the okra, cutting off and disposing of the tops and cutting the rest into small chunks.

Put the oil or ghee into a frying pan and fry the fenugreek seeds for a minute or two before they turn brown. Then add the okra and the rest of the ingredients and cook for 10-15 minutes on a medium to low heat, stirring occasionally. Add a little water during cooking if needed.

The dish can be served with plain rice or as part of a combination of other vegetarian 'mezze' dishes.

# POTATO SUBJI

This is a fairly light potato dish that can help to reduce pitta and vata if not too many hot spices are added, but can slightly increase kapha.

4 medium size potatoes
3 tablespoons of ghee or vegetable oil
1 teaspoon of cumin
½ teaspoon of turmeric
1 teaspoon of black mustard seeds
1 pinch of cayenne pepper
½ teaspoon of salt
2 teaspoons of coriander powder (or chopped fresh coriander)

Peel and chop the potatoes into small cubes, then boil in a saucepan of water until they are soft.

Meanwhile, put the oil or ghee to a frying pan and bring to a medium heat, before adding and frying all the dry spices for a few minutes.

Then drain the potatoes and stir them into the fried spice mixture, cooking for another couple of minutes while stirring.

This dish is great served on its own, or with other vegetable curry dishes or yoghurt.

# SPICY TOFU

For vegans who want to introduce more protein into their diet, this is a fairly substantial and heavy dish that can increase kapha, but reduce pitta and vata.

1 pound (1/2 kg) firm tofu
3 tablespoons of vegetable oil (ghee can be used for non-vegans)
1 teaspoon black mustard seeds
1 teaspoon cumin seeds
1 finely chopped chili pepper
2 cloves crushed garlic
1/2 teaspoon turmeric
1 teaspoon of dry coriander
1 small chopped onion

Heat the oil or ghee in a frying pan and add the cumin and mustard seeds and fry until they pop and are cooked.

Add the onion, garlic and the rest of the spices and gently fry until the onions are soft and brown.

Chop the tofu into small chunks and add slowly to the fried spice mix, then stir and let if cook for a few minutes until the tofu is hot and has absorbed all the spices. Add a little water if the mix is too dry.

It can be served with rice or Indian breads.

# CUCUMBER RAITA

This refreshing yoghurt dish is a great accompaniment to spicy Indian foods (a similar dish is also seen in Greek cuisine, called Tzatziki). As a watery, cooling dish it is good for pitta and vata but can increase kapha.

2 medium size cucumbers
½ teaspoon cumin seeds
1 small handful of curry leaves
½ teaspoon of black mustard seeds
½ teaspoon of dry coriander (or chopped fresh coriander)
I pinch cayenne pepper
3 tablespoons of ghee or vegetable oil
1 cup of natural yogurt

Heat the ghee or oil in a frying pan on a medium heat and add the mustard and cumin seeds. Cook until the seeds pop then add the rest of the dry ingredients and fry for a few more minutes. Then take the pan off the heat to cool.

Skin and grate the cucumber into a bowl and try to remove all the excess moisture, perhaps using paper towel. Add the yogurt and mix together, before adding the cold spice mix made earlier. Mix everything together and then it is ready to serve, or can be left chilled in the fridge until needed.

It makes a perfect accompaniment to hot curries, or served as a dip with Indian breads.

# COCONUT MACAROONS

Here's a sweet recipe to finish off on, to give you a complete ayurvedic menu. As a sweet food, it will increase kapha, but reduce pitta and vata. (The maple and rice syrups used can be substituted with normal sugar or sugar syrup if necessary.)

4 egg whites
4 oz powdered almonds
½ teaspoon baking powder
12 oz shredded coconut
4 oz maple syrup
4 oz brown rice syrup
¼ teaspoon cream of tartar

Beat the egg whites and cream of tartar until the mix is stiff enough to form soft peaks. In another bowl, combine all the other ingredients and mix thoroughly. Then carefully fold in the egg white mix.

Form the completed mixture into small balls and place them on a greased baking sheet or onto rice paper which can be eaten with them.

Bake for around 20-30 minutes or until golden brown, in a medium oven at 170 deg C (150 deg C in a fan oven).

# CHAPTER SIX

# Ayurveda, Life and Death

A person's age and stage in life is also important in ayurvedic thinking, which divides the human lifespan into different stages, which are taken into account when therapies are prescribed.

The first of these, is the 'bala' stage, which extends from childhood into young adulthood and where we are learning and discovering ourselves as well as the world around us. This period of life is dominated by kapha as the watery dosha which helps to create life.

The next stage is from young adult to middle age, known as the 'madhya vaya' stage. This is when we concentrate on work and building up our wealth, as well as bringing up children if we decide to have them. As the most active phase of life this is dominated by the fiery pitta dosha and our focus on our spiritual growth may be limited, as we focus most of our energies on work and family.

The third stage is 'jirna vaya'. It is a time when our work and family duties may be reducing. Our children may be grown up and our focus may be moving towards retirement and later life. It is seen as a transition stage between pitta and vata in our lives, when we start to have a more spiritual and less materialistic focus.

Towards the end of this phase we are preparing for death and thinking about being reborn into a new life. We think back over

our life and at this time we should learn how to forgive people and amend any wrongs we may have done.

This period is dominated by vata, the dosha most related to decay. At this stage, we may lose interest in the material affairs of life and think more about our spiritual destination.

These stages can be longer or shorter depending on the person, with some people staying in an infantile stage for a long time, just liking to have fun and not thinking about the future, while others may get stuck in the mid-life pitta stage and be focused on wealth and material possessions well into old age.

As with Western doctors, ayurvedic doctors are often most focused on the very young and very old, since these are the stages when we are most vulnerable to illnesses.

When it comes to children, in the kapha or watery stage of life, many illnesses can be related to the areas of the body with watery substances such as mucus and phlegm. So, illnesses in the lungs, throat or nose, where excess mucus then builds up, can be very common in children and these are seen as kapha type illnesses.

Old age is dominated by the vata dosha, the air humor, with its qualities of dryness and decay. General illnesses of a vata nature related to old age include skin problems, brittle bones and loss of hair, as well as reduction in the senses such as seeing and hearing. Ayurvedic treatments can use diet to help with the effects of ageing with, for instance, the herb ashwagandha often used to strengthen bones and joints. Also, aloe gel is seen as a good treatment for ageing skin, to keep it smooth and moisturized.

Above all, old age is seen as a time when we should be developing our spiritual side and concentrating less on our achievements in life and material wealth. This is one area where modern Western culture could learn a lot from ayurvedic thinking, since the focus in our culture is on youth and materialism, with less respect given to the elderly and their wisdom. Also, many older people are not as wise as they could be because they cling onto the traits of youth and don't develop their spirituality.

# The Afterlife

In the ancient vedic texts, there are two paths that can be taken after death. Most people will follow the path of the ancestors, where they are taken to a heaven occupied by their ancestors and will later be reborn to live through another life, one which may be influenced by their previous life. So, for instance, any bad karma (bad actions) in one life may influence the situation or character you are born into in a new life.

In the Hindu religion, there are many heavens and hells where a person's soul and 'jiva' (subtle being) can go, depending on the karma they created in life, which may also affect the period of time they stay there before being reborn.

The second path is the path of the gods, where an enlightened person may enter into the light of universal consciousness, a concept which also exists in many different religions and philosophies that have been influenced by ancient vedic thinking. For instance, in Buddhism this state of enlightenment is called Nirvana or Santori. Once here, the soul has escaped the circle of life and death, so will not be reborn.

Vedic thinking sees life and death as part of a continual process for the soul, with both life and the period resting in heaven being temporary.

In Hinduism, the soul and Jiva and can live through many lives in many different bodies, with the challenges of each life and the karma built up during each life, having an influence on the next life.

Hindus should not fear death, as it is not seen as an ending but part of a continual process. This even influenced Hindu warriors in the past, who entered the battlefield with the aim of fighting to the death so that they would then enter the heaven reserved for warriors, called Vira-Svargam.

Hindus are normally cremated, not buried, and this links back to the main concept in ayurveda that the body is made up of the five elements of 'prakriti' (nature) which are the same ones used to define the doshas, namely fire, earth, water, air and ether.

By cremating the body, these five elements within it are all released and returned to their respective spheres, at the same time releasing the subtle body (jiva) and the soul to continue the journey into the afterlife.

# Final Thoughts

I hope this book has been an informative introduction to ayurveda for those who are new to the subject. As a yoga and mindfulness meditation teacher, I am constantly drawing on aspects of ayurveda, whether it be recommending a diet to suit one of my students, with reference to their particular dosha type, or telling them about some of the simpler ayurvedic herbs and remedies that they can use themselves.

I also tell them about other ayurvedic treatments such as gem therapy and I have always enjoyed discovering and exploring different types of therapies, to see which are the most effective.

If you plan to travel to India in the future, I would certainly recommend seeking out a qualified ayurveda doctor, for a full analysis of your dosha type and help with any illnesses you may have. Some ayurveda doctors have also set up practice in other countries, so it may be worth looking to see if there are any that are closer to where you live.

Above all, I wish you good health and happiness in your life and on your spiritual journey.

# Index

**A**

afterlife 150–1

agni 52–9

aim mantra 109

akash 20, 40

alochaka pitta 28–9

apana vata 27

ashti dhatu 22

astringent taste 46–7, 50, 51, 56, 58

Atharvaveda 6

avalambaka kapha 31

ayurveda

.............author's experience of 9–10

....................as complete system 7–9

.........................................as complementary medicine 10–12

conflicts with modern medicine 12, 14–17

.....................................and dhatus 21–4

.....................and doshas 20–1, 25–39

.............................five elements in 20

...........................................texts for 6–7

.......................and seven tissues 21–4

**B**

bala stage 146

balanced agni 55

basti 81, 84

bhrajaka pitta 28, 29

bitter taste 45, 51, 56

Black Lentil Dal 132–3

blue sapphire 98

bodhaka kapha 31

body shapes 76–7

**C**

cat's eye 98

Charaka Samhita 7

Coconut Macaroons 142–3

crown chakra 121, 125

Cucumber Raita 140–1

**D**

Dhanvantra Mantra 106

dhatus 21–4

diamond 96, 98

diet 128–43

digestive fire 52–9

doshas 20–1, 25–39, 47–9, 70–2

**E**

emerald 96

**F**

five elements 20, 40

**G**

gandharva massage 114

Gayatri Mantra 106, 107, 108

gem therapy 93–100

gunas 62–73

**H**

heart chakra 121, 123–4

heera 96, 98

high agni 56

hrim mantra 109

hum mantra 109

**J**

jala 20, 40

jirna vaya stage 146

**K**

kapha dosha

..........................................and agni 56, 58

.............. and astringent taste 46, 50

................................ and bitter taste 45

............................... description of 30–1

............................................................

and diet 129, 130, 131, 132, 134, 136, 138, 140, 142

.......... as dominant dosha 35, 37, 39

............. and gem therapy 95, 96, 98

.............................................as humor 20

....................... and life stages 146, 148

...........and massage therapy 112, 114

...................................................................

and oil and herb therapy 87–8, 89

.......... and pungent taste 44, 50, 51

..............and reduction therapies 76

...................................and salty taste 42

............................ and seven tissues 22

........................ and sour taste 42–3, 51

..............and sweet taste 41, 47–8, 51

kledaka kapha 31

**L**

life stages 146, 148–9

low agni 55–6

**M**

madhya vaya stage 146

majja dhatu 22

mamsa dhatu 22

manakya 95

manda agni 55–6

mantra therapy 104–9

marma abhyanga massage 113

massage therapy 110–14

meda dhatu 22

meditation therapy 101–3

mukta 95

**N**

nasya 81, 84–5

neelam 96

**O**

oil and herb therapy 87–92

om mantra 108

**P**

pachaka pitta 28, 29

pallation therapy 79

Pan-Fried Okra 134–5

pancha karma 9–10, 80–6

panna 96

pearl 95

pitta dosha

........................................and agni 56, 58

.......................and astringent taste 46

................................. and bitter taste 45

.............................. description of 28–9

..............................................................

and diet 128, 129, 130, 132, 134, 136, 138, 140, 142

..........as dominant dosha 35, 37, 39

.............and gem therapy 95, 96, 98

.............................................as humor 20

........................and life stages 146, 148

............ and massage therapy 111, 113

.....and oil and herb therapy 88, 89

...........................and pungent taste 44

.................................and salty taste 42

..............................................................

and seven tissues 23, 42–3, 44, 45, 46, 46, 56

.............................and sour taste 42–3

........................and sweet taste 41, 48

Potato Subji 136–7

prana vata 27

pranayama 118–20

praval 95–6

prithi 20, 40

pungent taste 44–5, 50, 51, 56, 58

purification therapy 79

**Q**

quartz crystal 99

**R**

rajas guna 62–3, 65, 67, 69, 71, 72

rakta dhatu 22

rakta moksha 81, 85

ranjaka pitta 28, 29

rasa dhatu 22

red coral 95–6

reduction therapies 76, 79

*Rigveda* 6

root chakra 121, 122–3

ruby 95

**S**

sacral chakra 121, 123

sadhaka pitta 28

salty taste 42, 50, 51, 56, 58

sama agni 55

samana vata 27

*Samaveda* 6

sattva guna 62, 63 66, 68, 70, 71, 72

seven chakras 121–5

seven tissues 21–4

sham mantra 109

shirodhara massage 112

shukra dhatu 22

six tastes 40–51, 129–30

six tastes pill 48–9

sleshaka kapha 31

solar-plexus chakra 121, 123

sour taste 42–3, 51, 56, 58

sphatic 99

Spicy Tofu 138–9

Sushruta Samhita 7

sweet taste 41, 47–8, 50–1, 56, 57, 58, 59

**T**

tamas guna 63, 65, 67, 69, 71

tarpaka kapha 31

tejas 20, 40

third eye chakra 121, 124

throat chakra 121, 124

tikshna agni 56

tonification therapies 76, 77–8

trigunas 62–73

**U**

udvartana massage 114

**V**

vaidurya 98

vamana 81, 82–3

variable agni 55

vata dosha

........................................and agni 55, 58

......................and astringent taste 46

...............................and bitter taste 45

..............................description of 25–7

and diet 129, 130, 132, 134, 136, 138, 140, 142

.........as dominant dosha 34, 36, 38

.............and gem therapy 95, 96, 98

...........................................as humor 20

.......................and life stages 146, 148

...................and massage therapy 111

......and oil and herb therapy 87, 89

...................and pungent taste 44, 51

..................................and salty taste 42

.......................and seven tissues 22–3

.......................and sour taste 42–3, 51

.................and sweet taste 41, 48, 51

...........and tonification therapies 76

vayu 20, 40

Verma, Virendra 9

virechana 81, 83

vishama agni 55

VPK type 32

vyana vata 27

*Yajurveda* 6

yoga 118–25

# About the Author

Konstantinos Tselios is a Greekborn mindfulness and yoga teacher, now based in both London and on the Greek island of Crete, He is also a magazine journalist, writing about yoga and alternative health and spirituality, with a series of features published in Kindred Spirit and Prediction magazines in the UK.

He has travelled widely, with many trips to India over the past 20 years, gaining some of his yoga teaching qualifications there (he is fully qualified as a teacher in Shivananda Yoga, Agama Yoga and Jivamukti Yoga). He is also a qualified mindfulness teacher, carrying out classes in person as well as online.

In 2014, Kostas was diagnosed with Stage 4 bowel cancer, requiring an emergency operation, followed up by chemotherapy. This made him even more interested in complementary medicines and various natural cancer-beating health protocols, which he used as part of his own recovery.

This health and dietary advice is now something he passes on to students, including ayurvedic health knowledge gained from his long-term friendship with his Indian ayurveda doctor Virendra Verma, who is based in Varanasi in India.

Konstantinos can be contacted at: costastselios@yahoo.com

# Acknowledgements

The author would like to thank those who helped with this book, including Steve Rowe for his editing work, Joan Rowe for her copy-checking skills, plus Tania O'Donnell for making it all happen. He would also like to thank the Arcturus design team, led by Peter Ridley, and Dani Leigh for the beautiful design of the cover and the book. Thanks must also go to the many people and organizations that have helped him with his own health issues over the years, including the NHS health service in the UK, plus his ayurvedic doctor Virendra. He also thanks the many teachers and gurus who have guided him on his own spiritual path.